THE
HOW TO DRAW
Book For Kids

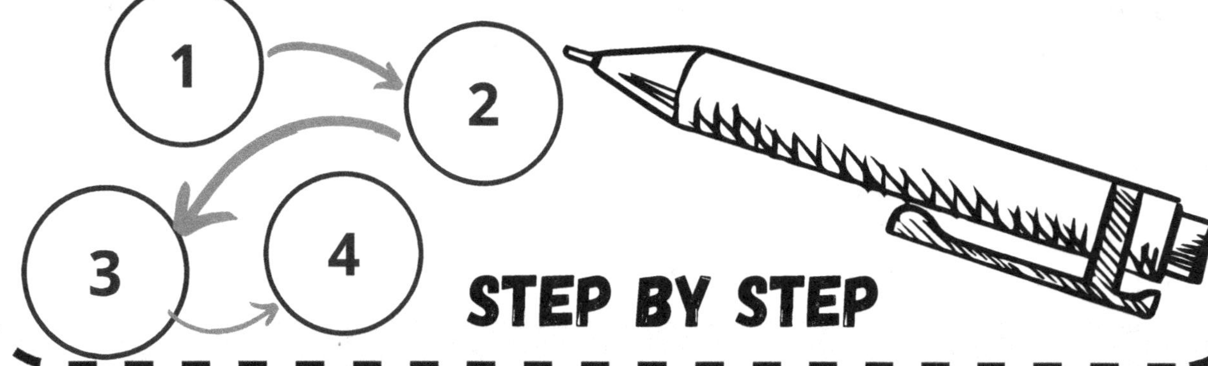

STEP BY STEP

HOW TO DRAW

STEP 1

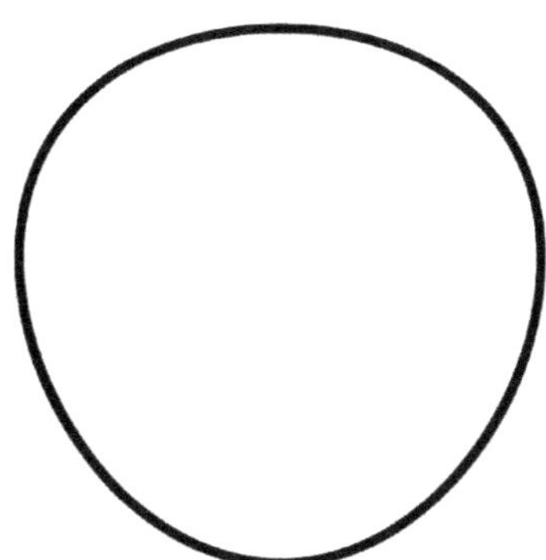

STEP 2

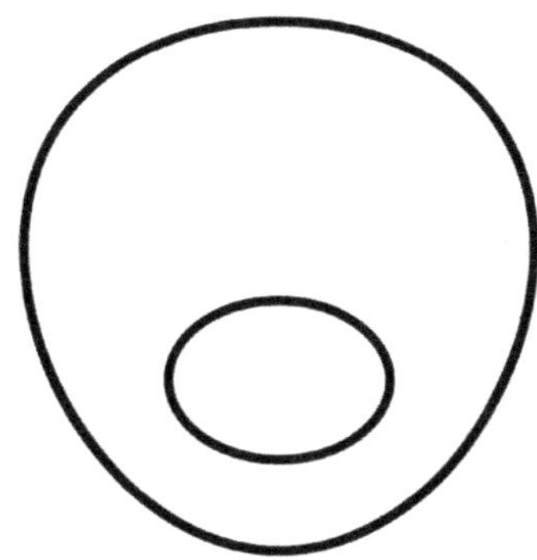

STEP 3

STEP 4

STEP 5

STEP6

HOW TO DRAW

STEP 1
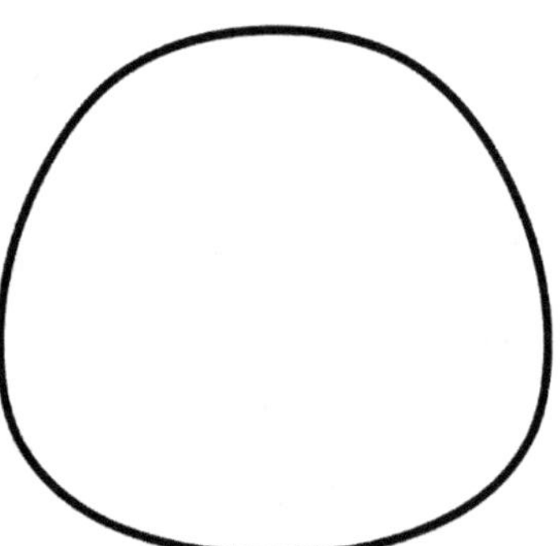

STEP 2
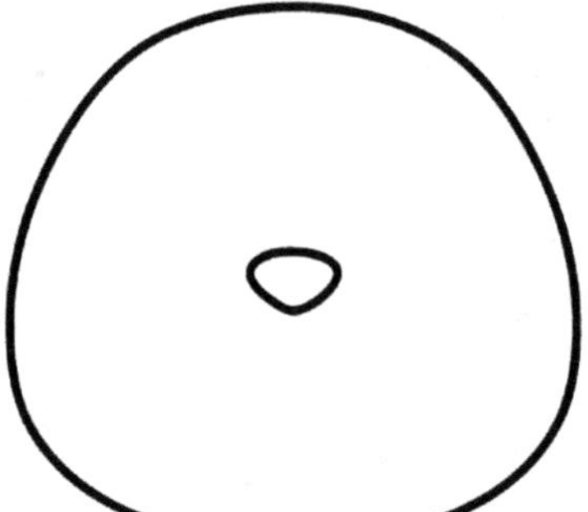

STEP 3

STEP 4

STEP 5

STEP6

HOW TO DRAW

STEP 1

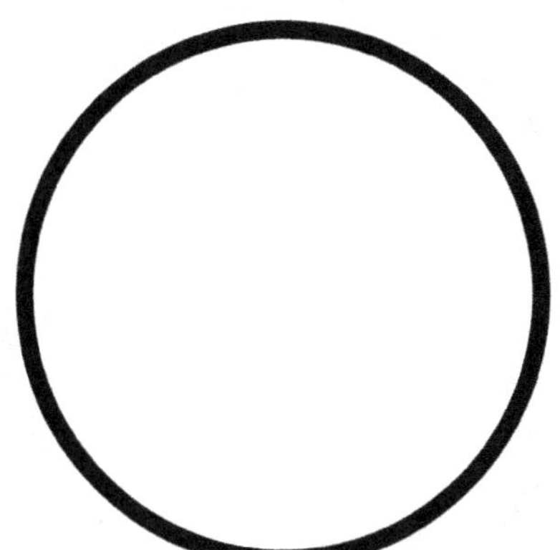

STEP 2

STEP 3

STEP 4

STEP 5

STEP 6

HOW TO DRAW

STEP 1

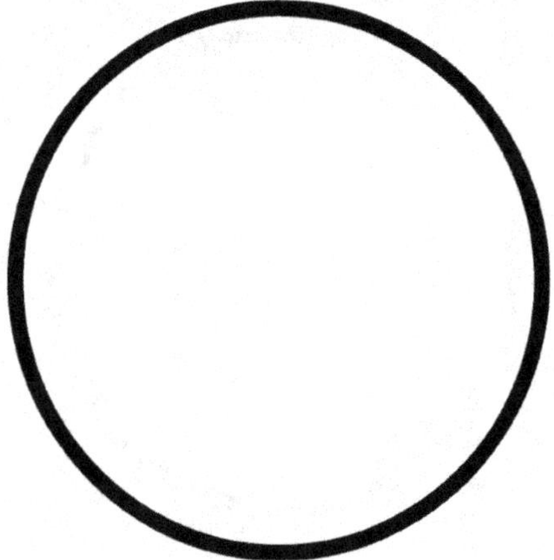

STEP 2

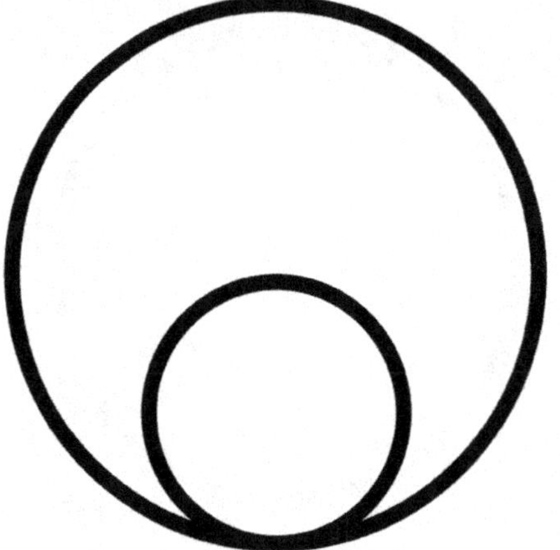

STEP 3

STEP 4

STEP 5

STEP 6

HOW TO DRAW

HOW TO DRAW

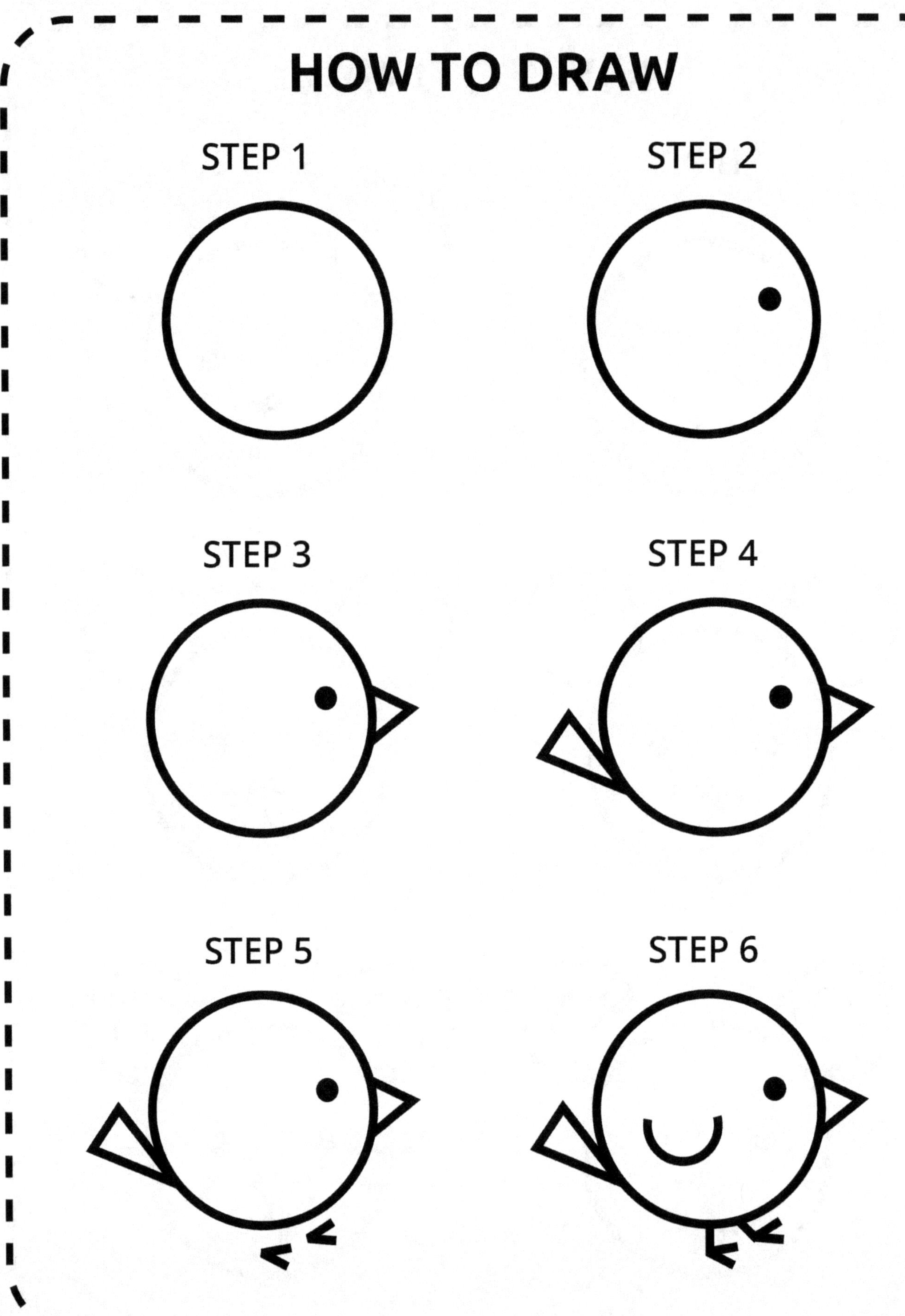

HOW TO DRAW

STEP 1

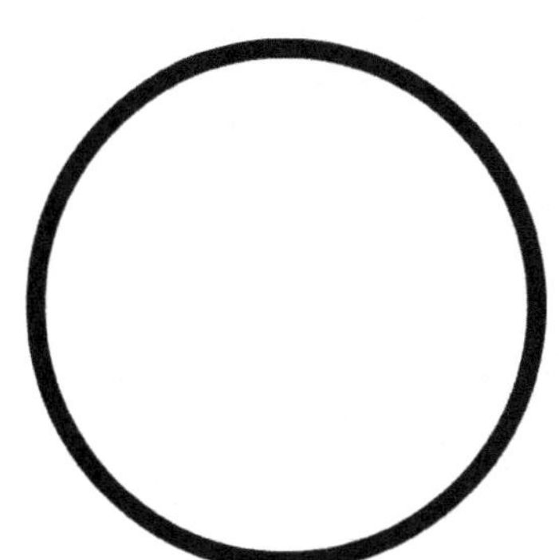

STEP 2

STEP 3

STEP 4

STEP 5

STEP 6

HOW TO DRAW

STEP 1

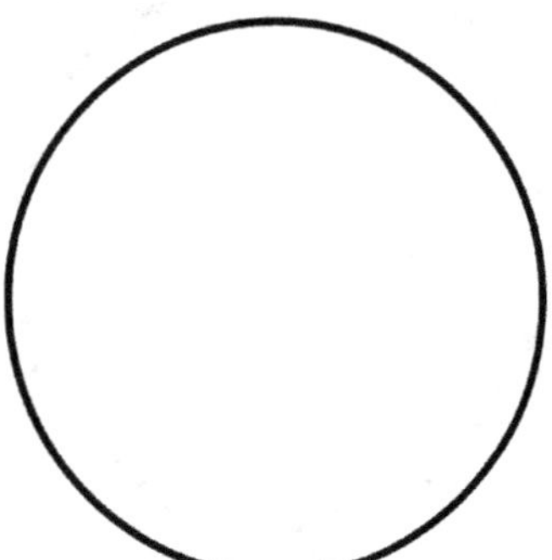

STEP 2

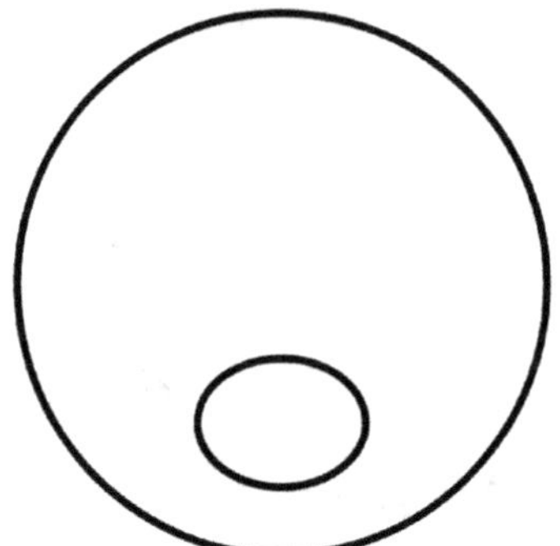

STEP 3

STEP 4

STEP 5

STEP6

HOW TO DRAW

STEP 1

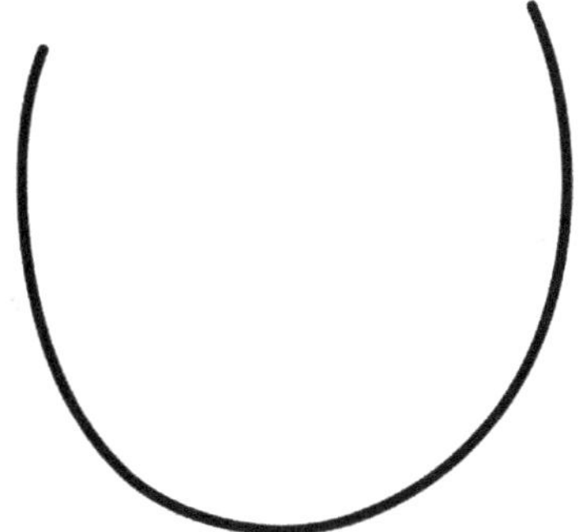

STEP 2

STEP 3

STEP 4

STEP 5

STEP6

HOW TO DRAW

STEP 1

STEP 2

STEP 3

STEP 4

STEP 5

STEP 6

HOW TO DRAW

STEP 1

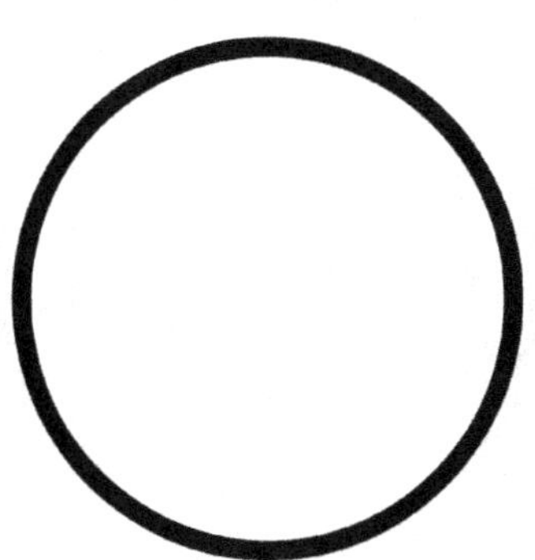

STEP 2

STEP 3

STEP 4

STEP 5

STEP 6

HOW TO DRAW

STEP 1

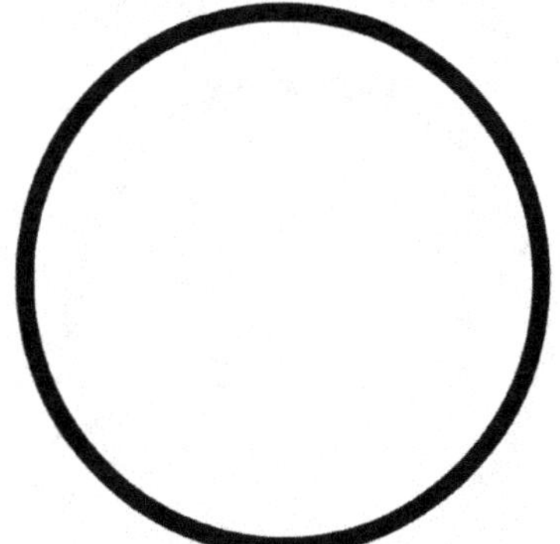

STEP 2

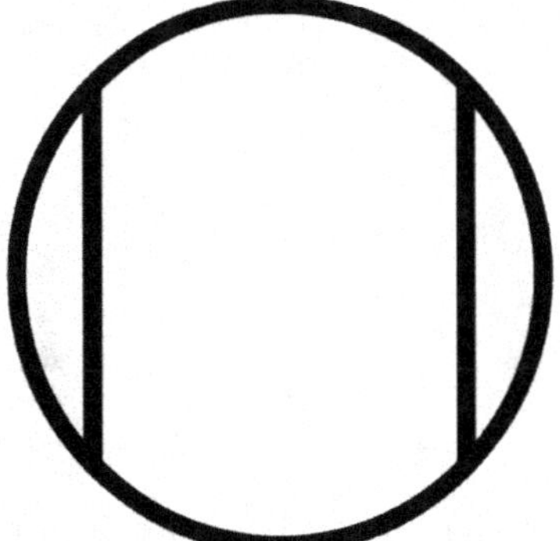

STEP 3

STEP 4

STEP 5

STEP 6

HOW TO DRAW

STEP 1

STEP 2

STEP 3

STEP 4

STEP 5

STEP 6

HOW TO DRAW

STEP 1

STEP 2

STEP 3

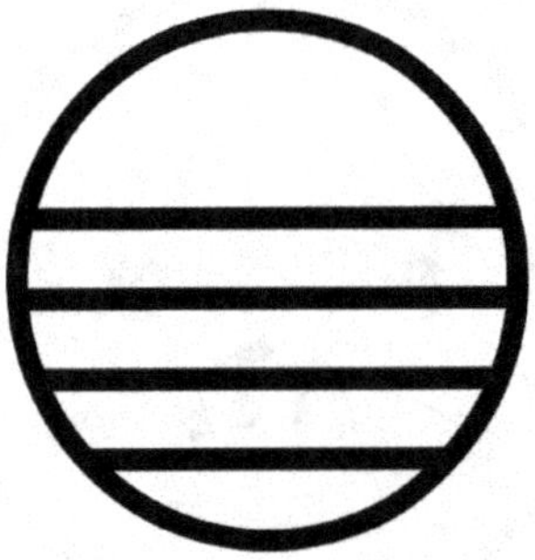

STEP 4

STEP 5

STEP 6

HOW TO DRAW

STEP 1

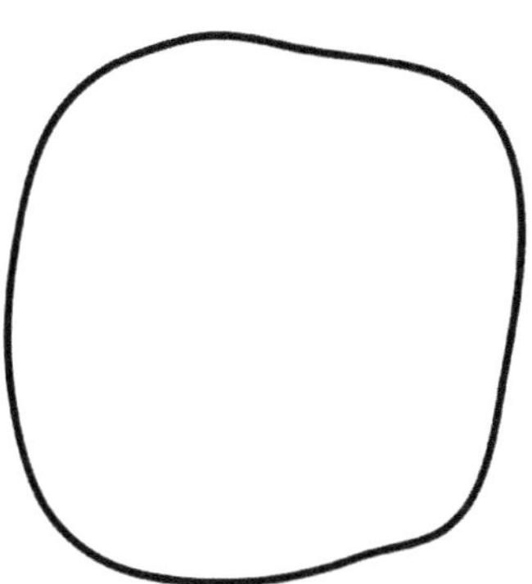

STEP 2

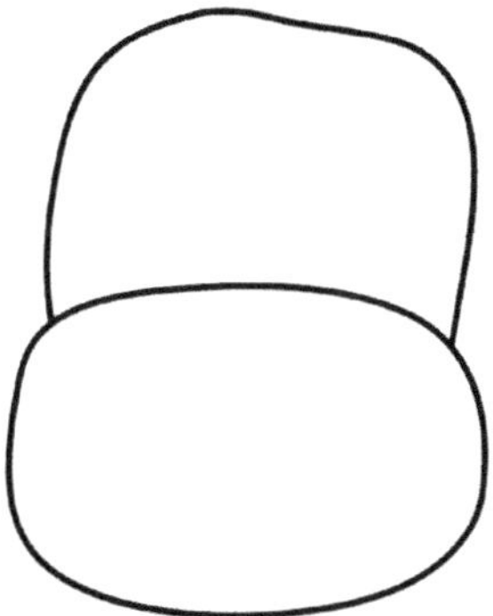

STEP 3

STEP 4

STEP 5

STEP6

HOW TO DRAW

STEP 1

STEP 2

STEP 3

STEP 4

STEP 5

STEP6

HOW TO DRAW

STEP 1

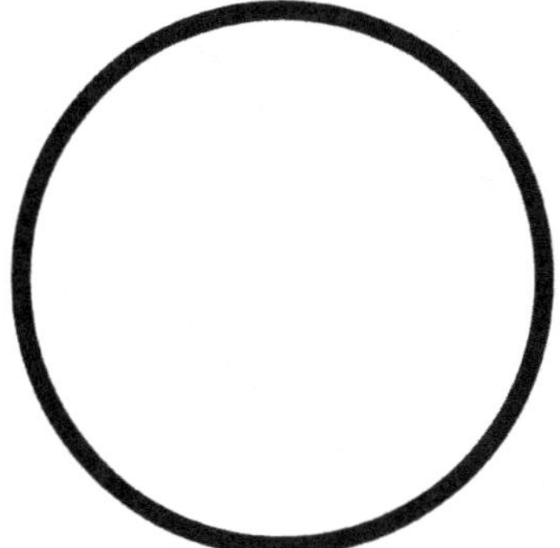

STEP 2

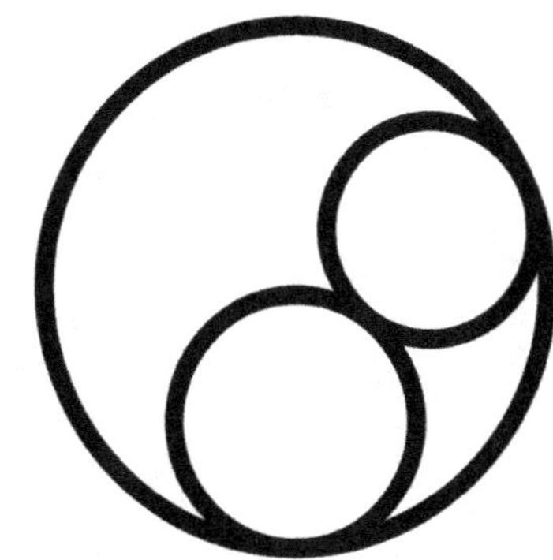

STEP 3

STEP 4

STEP 5

STEP 6

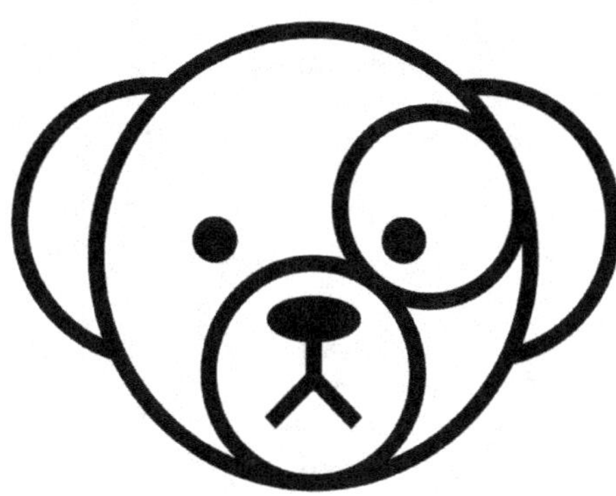

HOW TO DRAW

STEP 1

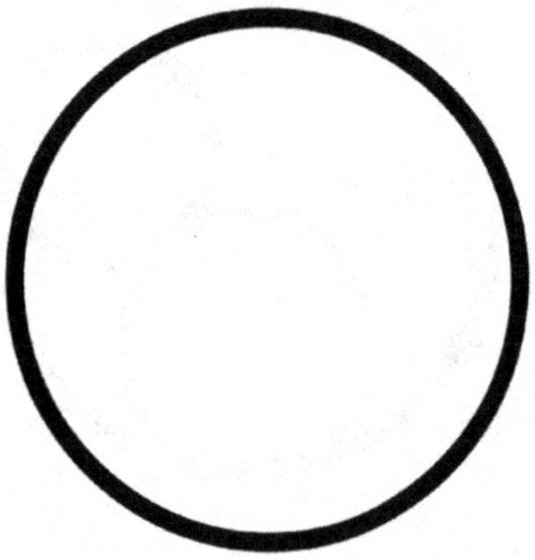

STEP 2

STEP 3

STEP 4

STEP 5

STEP 6

HOW TO DRAW

STEP 1

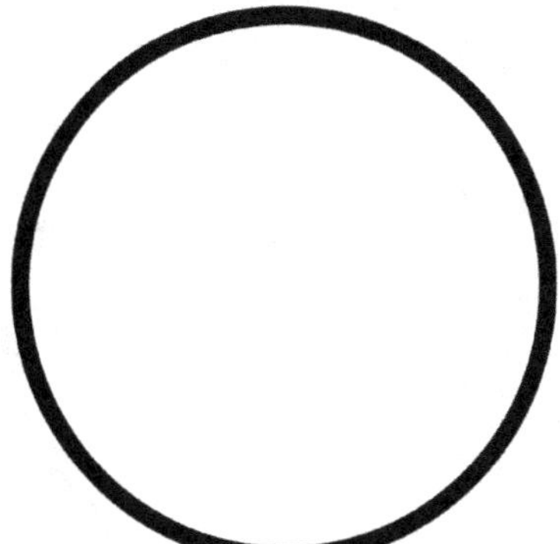

STEP 2

STEP 3

STEP 4

STEP 5

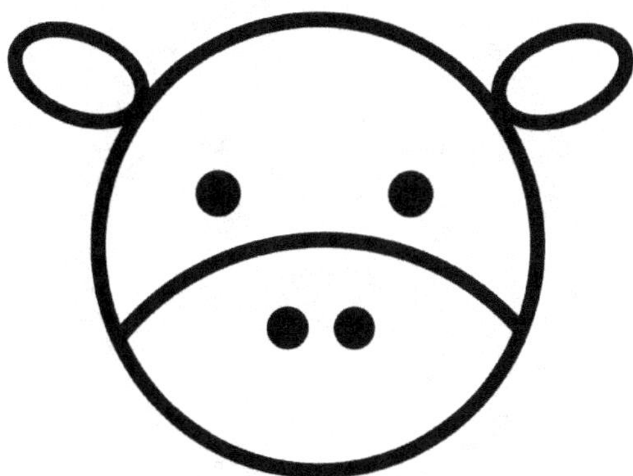

STEP 6

HOW TO DRAW

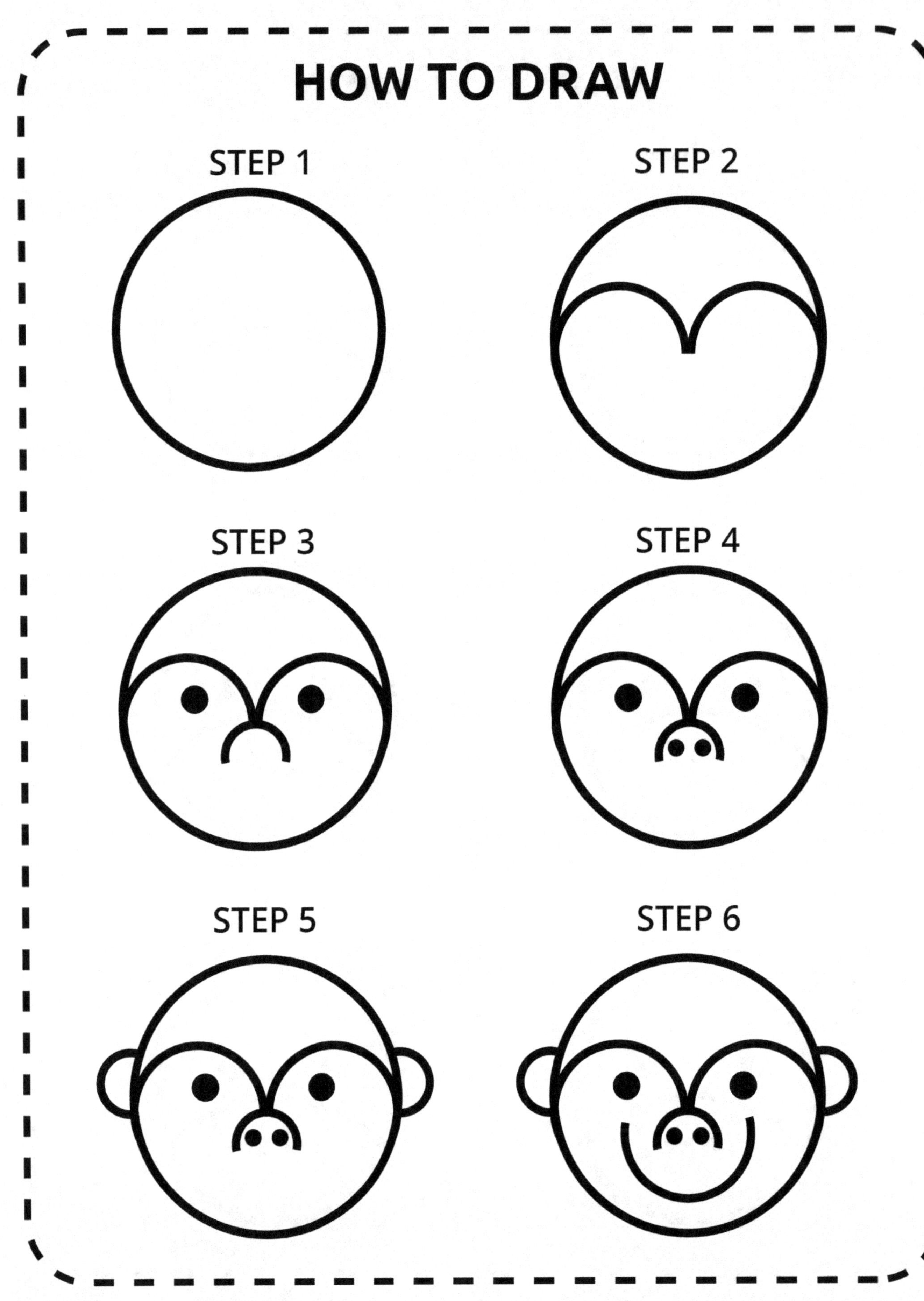

HOW TO DRAW

HOW TO DRAW

STEP 1

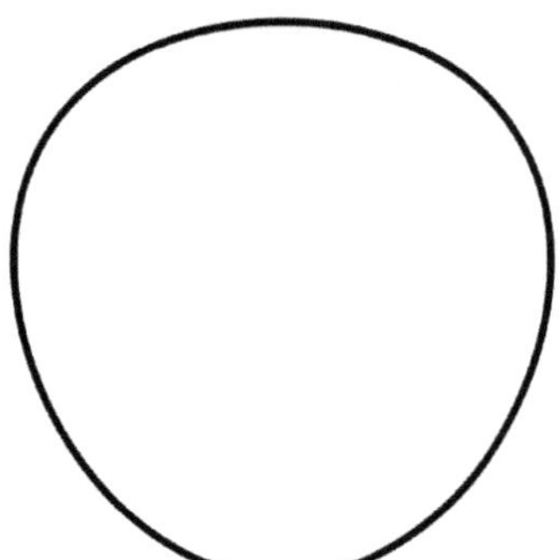

STEP 2

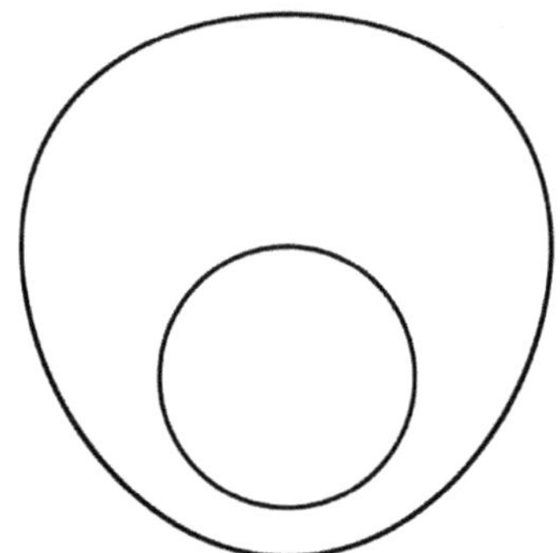

STEP 3

STEP 4

STEP 5

STEP6

HOW TO DRAW

STEP 1

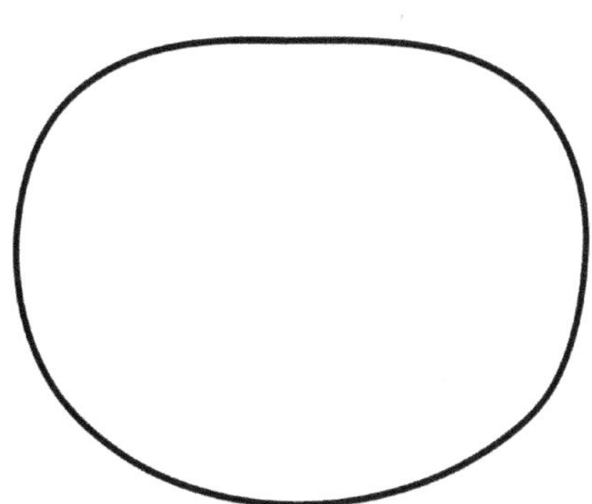

STEP 2

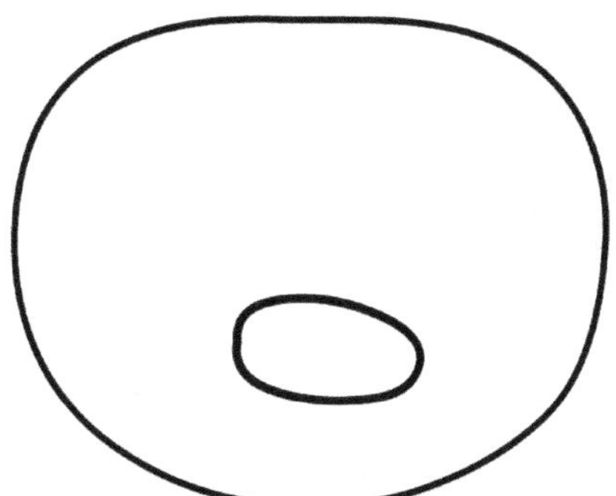

STEP 3

STEP 4

STEP 5

STEP6

HOW TO DRAW

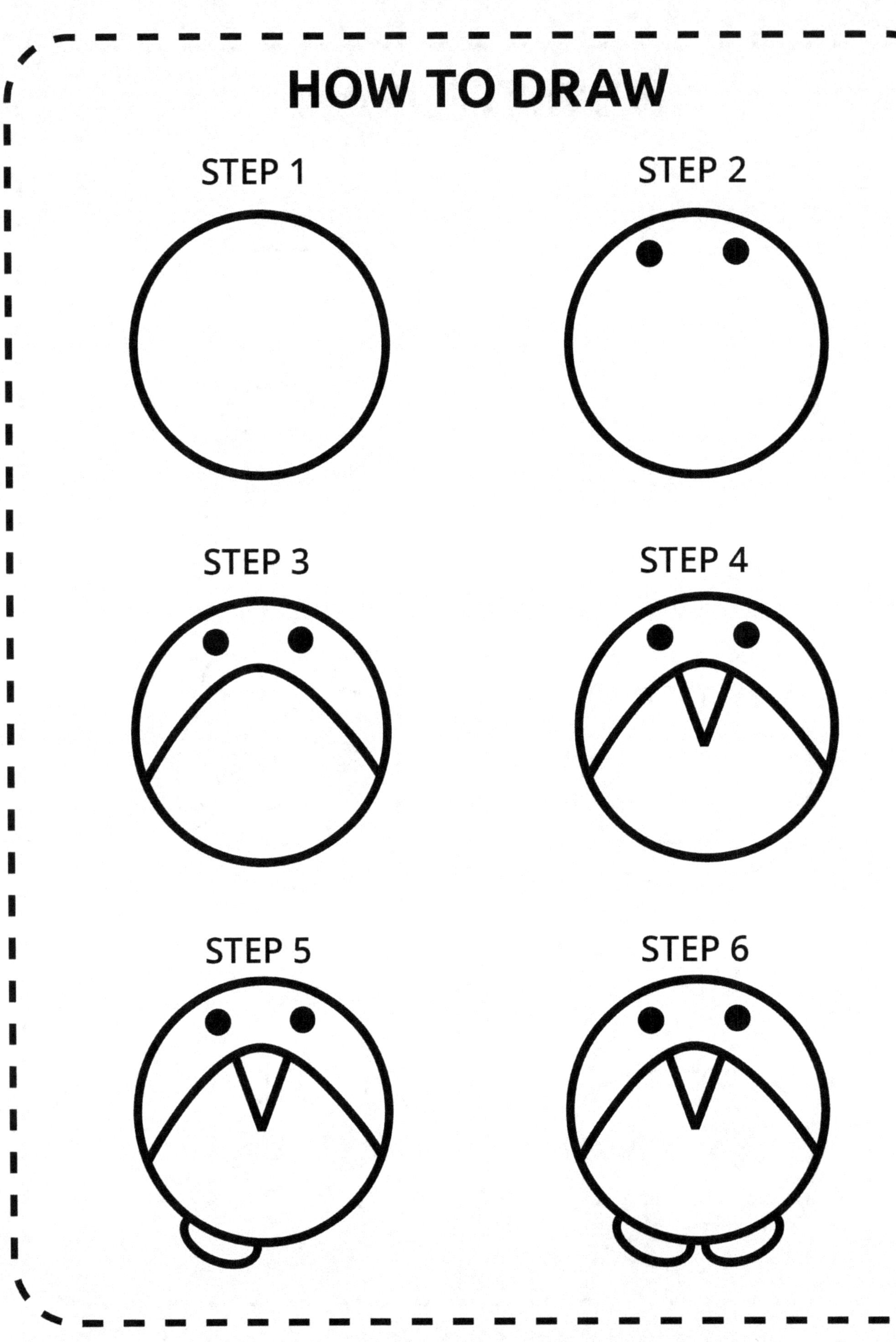

HOW TO DRAW

STEP 1

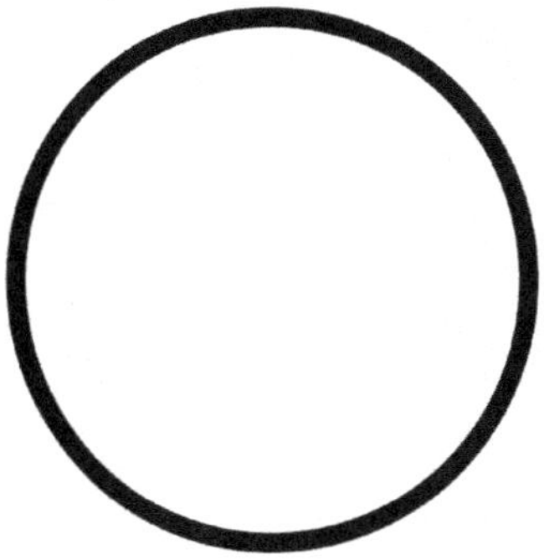

STEP 2

STEP 3

STEP 4

STEP 5

STEP 6

HOW TO DRAW

STEP 1

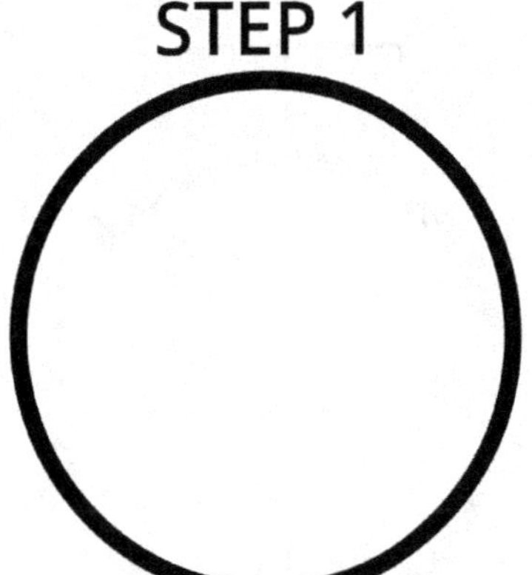

STEP 2

STEP 3

STEP 4

STEP 5

STEP 6

HOW TO DRAW

STEP 1

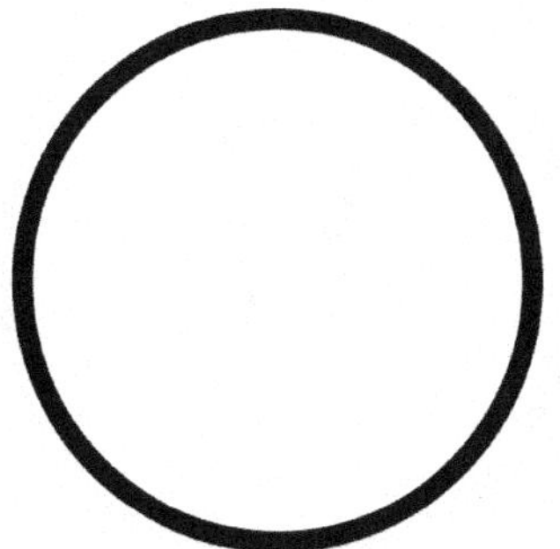

STEP 2

STEP 3

STEP 4

STEP 5

STEP 6

HOW TO DRAW

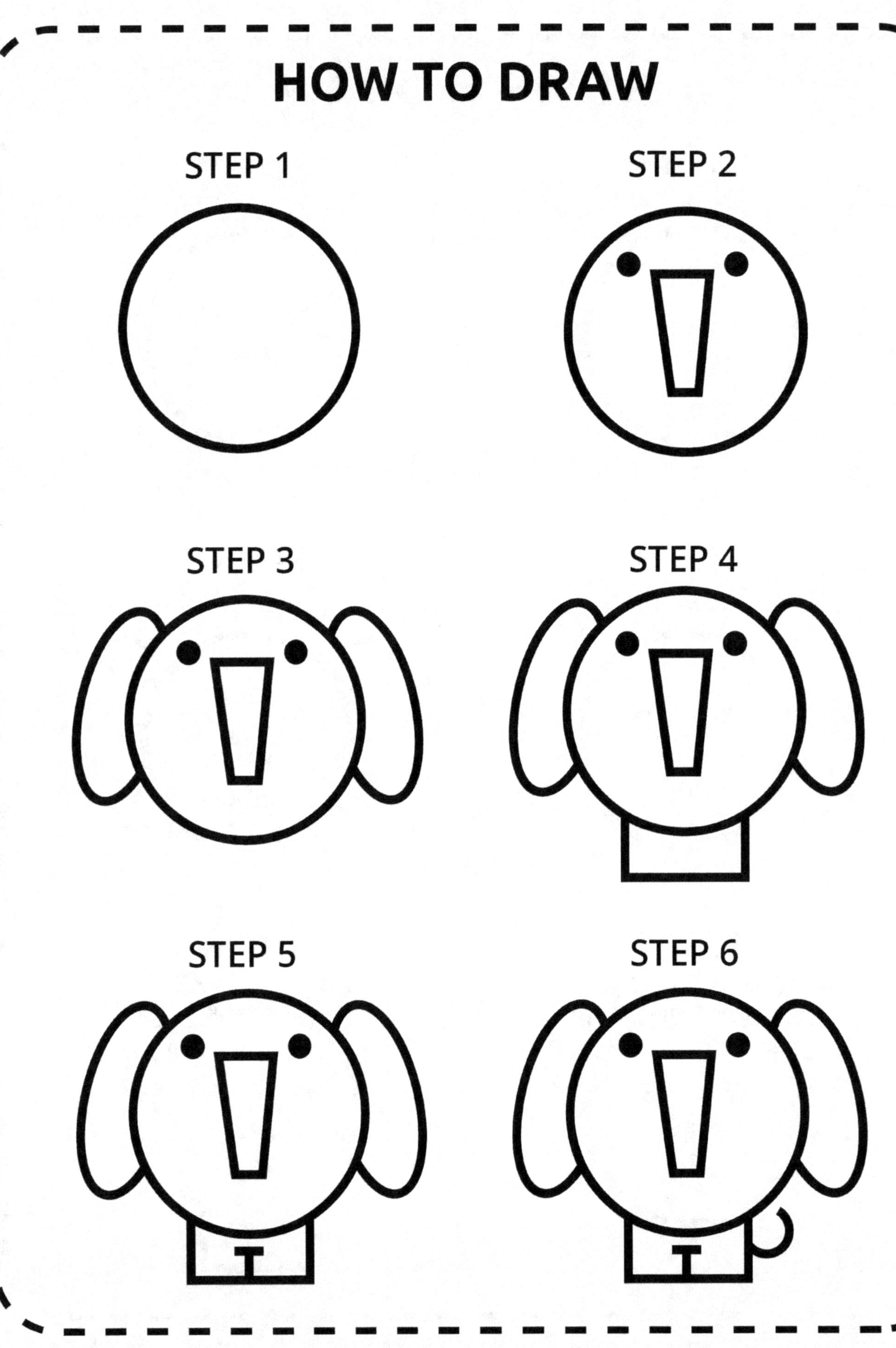

HOW TO DRAW

STEP 1

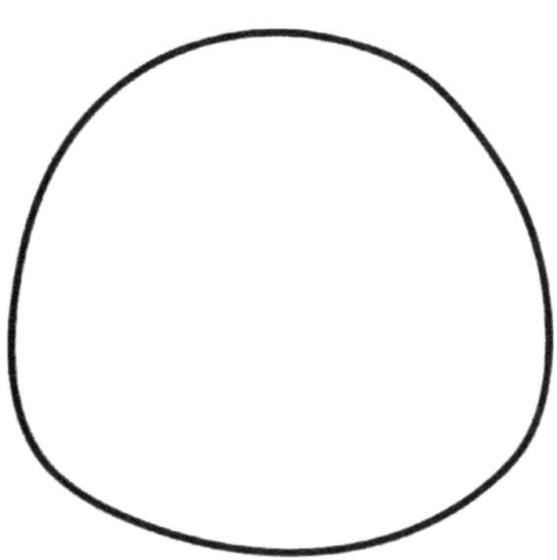

STEP 2

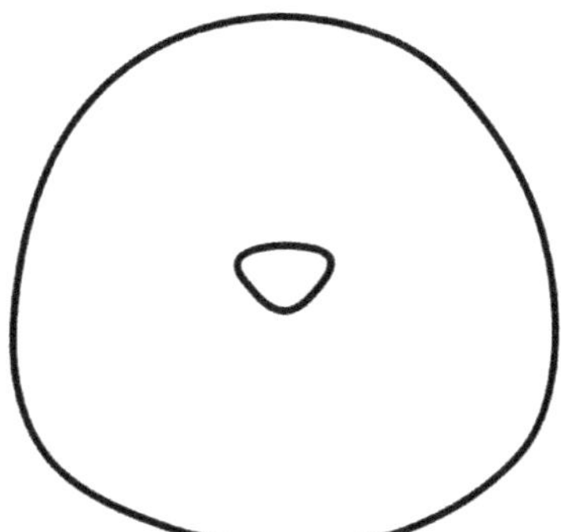

STEP 3

STEP 4

STEP 5

STEP6

HOW TO DRAW

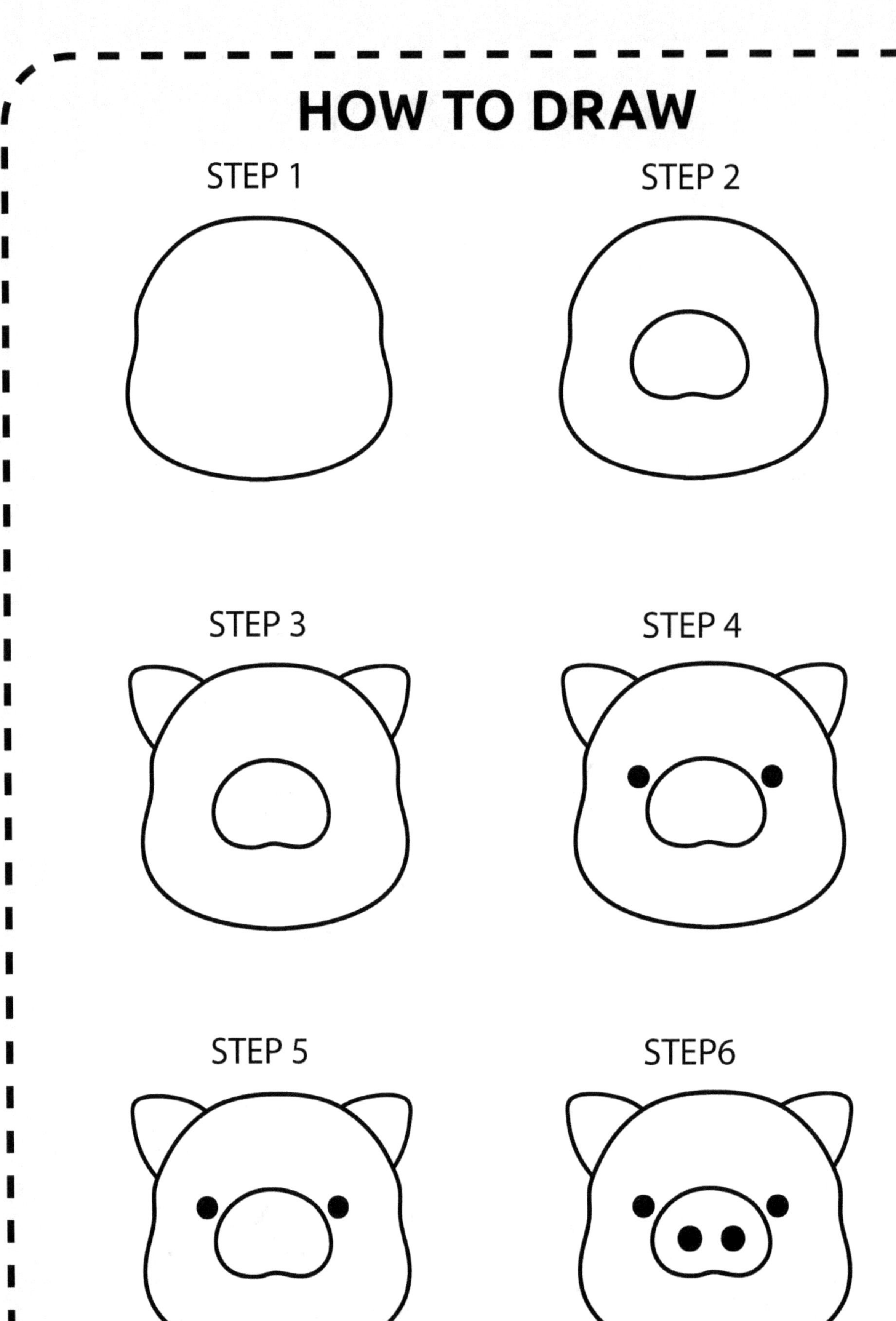

HOW TO DRAW

STEP 1
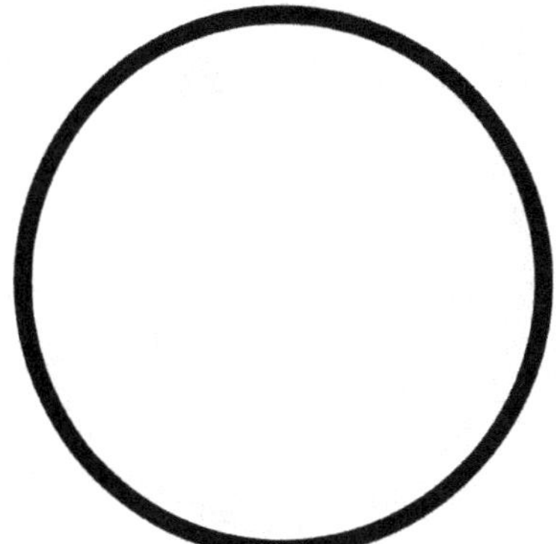

STEP 2

STEP 3

STEP 4

STEP 5

STEP 6

HOW TO DRAW

STEP 1

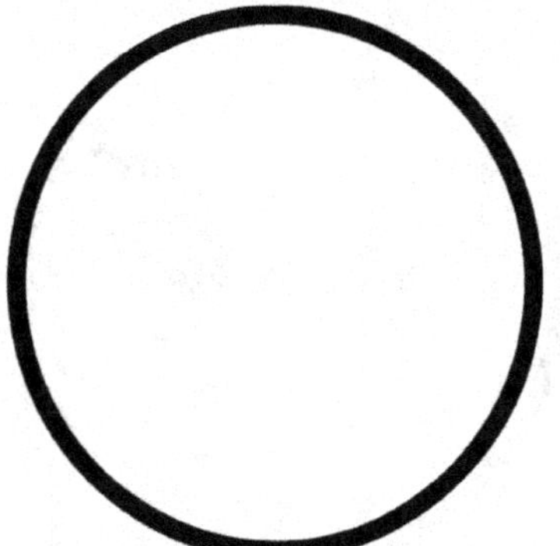

STEP 2

STEP 3

STEP 4

STEP 5

STEP 6

HOW TO DRAW

HOW TO DRAW

STEP 1

STEP 2

STEP 3

STEP 4

STEP 5

STEP 6

HOW TO DRAW

STEP 1

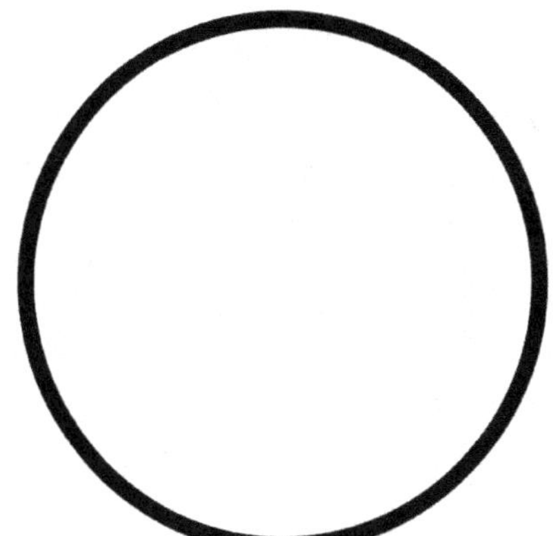

STEP 2

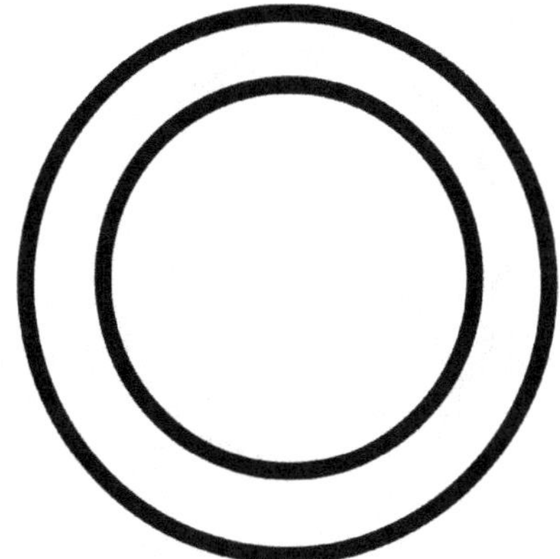

STEP 3

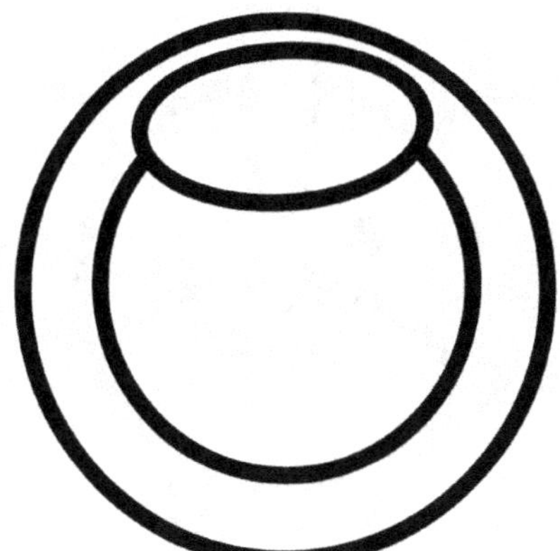

STEP 4

STEP 5

STEP 6

HOW TO DRAW

STEP 1

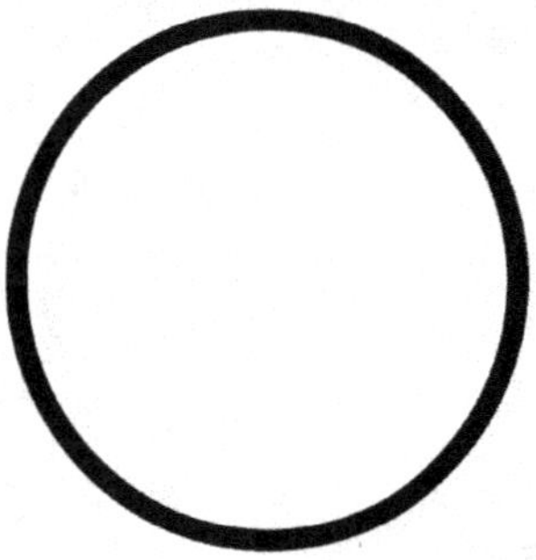

STEP 2

STEP 3

STEP 4

STEP 5

STEP 6

HOW TO DRAW

STEP 1

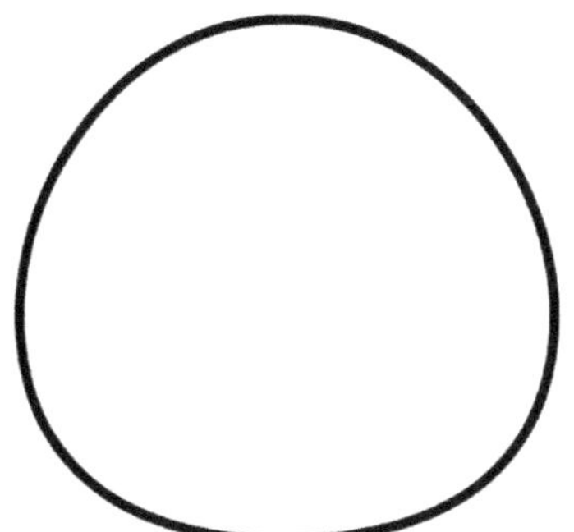

STEP 2

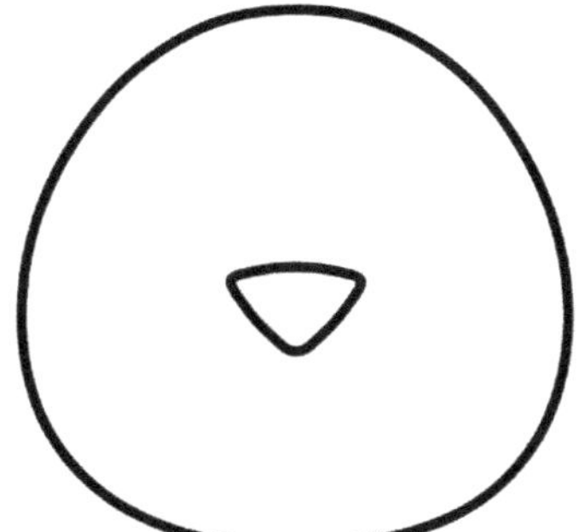

STEP 3

STEP 4

STEP 5

STEP6

HOW TO DRAW

STEP 1

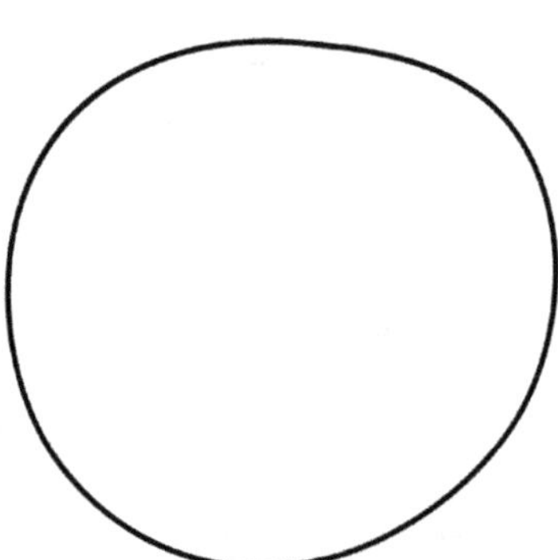

STEP 2

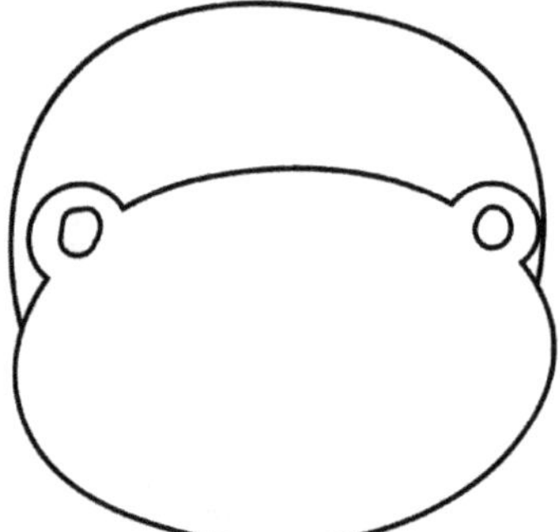

STEP 3

STEP 4

STEP 5

STEP6

HOW TO DRAW

STEP 1

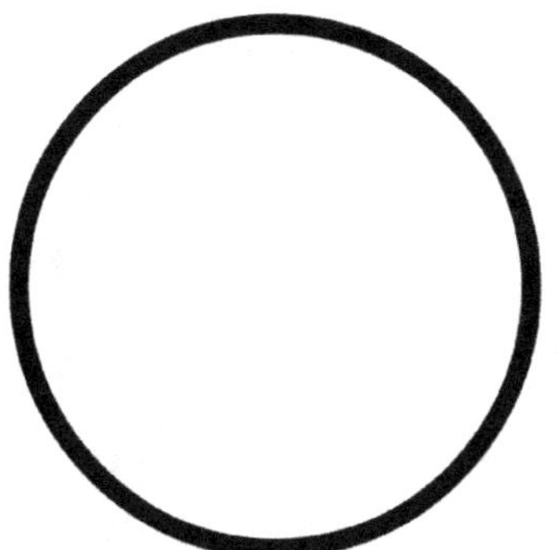

STEP 2

STEP 3

STEP 4

STEP 5

STEP 6

HOW TO DRAW

STEP 1

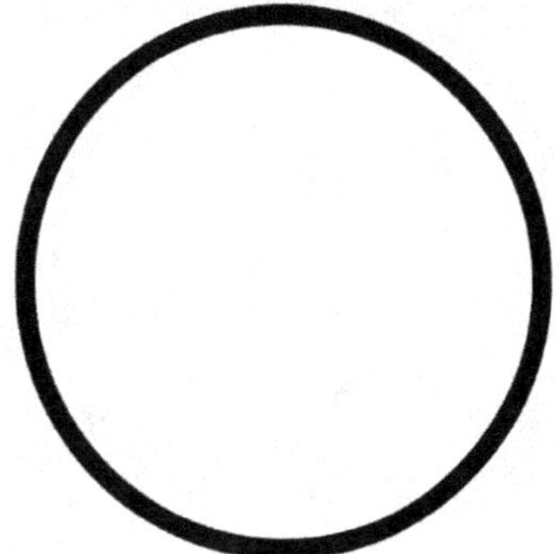

STEP 2

STEP 3

STEP 4

STEP 5

STEP 6

HOW TO DRAW

HOW TO DRAW

HOW TO DRAW

STEP 1
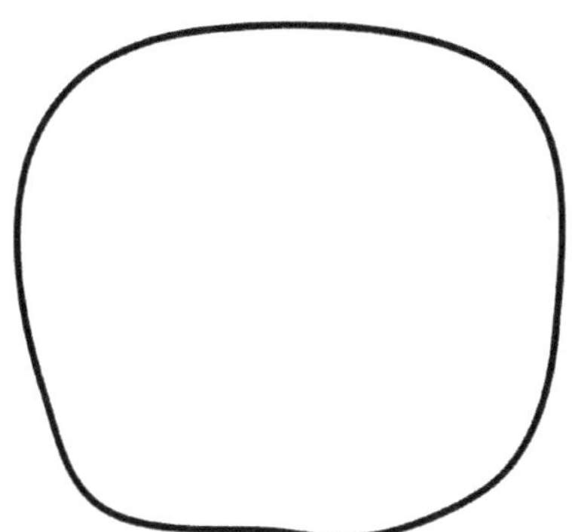

STEP 2

STEP 3

STEP 4

STEP 5

STEP6

HOW TO DRAW

STEP 1
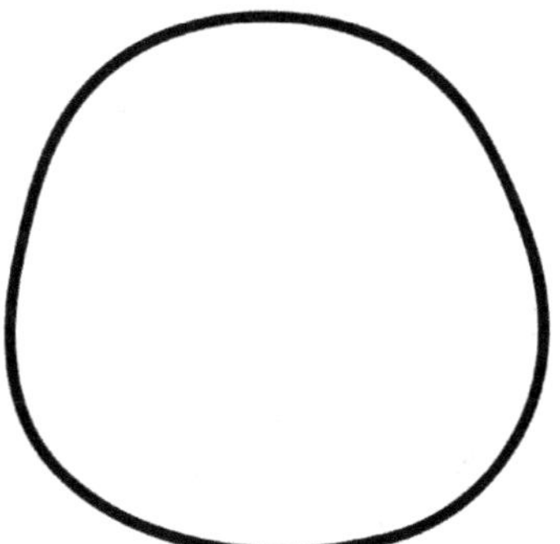

STEP 2

STEP 3

STEP 4

STEP 5

STEP6

Want to receive more FREE goodies?

Just email us at:
marissa.ostarrie.publishing@gmail.com

with title text:
Free Goodies + The title of the book

THANK YOU for choosing our book!
If you enjoy this book at all, a quick review on Amazon would really help us!

www.ingramcontent.com/pod-product-compliance
Lightning Source LLC
LaVergne TN
LVHW080613200726
843509LV00007B/297